THE VIRGINIA STATE
COLONY FOR EPILEPTICS
AND FEEBLEMINDED

THE VIRGINIA STATE COLONY FOR EPILEPTICS AND FEEBLEMINDED

POEMS

Molly McCully Brown

A Karen & Michael Braziller Book

PERSEA BOOKS / NEW YORK

Persea Books, Inc.
277 Broadway
New York, New York 10007

Library of Congress Cataloging-in-Publication Data
Names: Brown, Molly McCully, 1991– author.
Title: The Virginia State Colony for Epileptics and Feebleminded / Molly McMully Brown.
Description: First edition. | New York : Persea Books, 2017. | "Winner of the 2016 Lexi Rudnitsky First Book Prize in Poetry A Karen & Michael Braziller Book."

Identifiers: LCCN 2016037960 | ISBN 9780892554782 (original trade pbk. : alk=.paper)

Subjects: LCSH: State Colony for Epileptics and Feeble-Minded (Va.)—Poetry.=
| Epileptics—Poetry. | People with mental disabilities—Poetry.

Classification: LCC PS3602.R722354 A6 2017 | DDC 811/.6—dc23
LC record available at https://lccn.loc.gov/2016037960

Book design and composition by Rita Lascaro
Typeset in Garamond
Manufactured in the United States of America. Printed on acid-free paper.

for my parents

&

in memory of Frances:
always, everywhere

CONTENTS

PREFACE

The Virginia State Colony for Epileptics and Feebleminded opened in 1910 in Amherst County, Virginia, as the Virginia State Colony for Epileptics, a government-run residential hospital. In 1913, the facility also began serving patients it classified as "feebleminded" and by 1919 the name had been altered to reflect this fact. In 1924, the Colony became formally enmeshed with the Eugenics movement and began sterilizing, without their consent, patients it deemed "defectives." When, in 1927, the U.S. Supreme Court upheld Virginia sterilization laws in *Buck v. Bell,* eugenic sterilizations became an even more common practice. From the mid-1920s through the mid-1950s, more than 7,000 people were sterilized in Virginia, often without their knowledge. While some patients were sterilized and then released, others spent the better part of their lives at the Colony. Although the last eugenic sterilization is noted in the Colony's annual report for 1956, sterilizations may have continued into the 1970s.

THE VIRGINIA STATE
COLONY FOR EPILEPTICS
AND FEEBLEMINDED

THE CENTRAL VIRGINIA TRAINING CENTER

formerly The Virginia State Colony for Epileptics and Feebleminded

Whatever it is—
home or hospital,
graveyard or asylum,
government facility or great
tract of land slowly ceding
itself back to dust—

its church is a low-slung brick box
with a single window,
a white piece of plywood
labeled chapel, and a locked door.

Whatever it is,
my mother and I ride along
its red roads in February
with the windows down:
this place looks lived in,
that one has stiff, gray curtains
in the window, a roof caving in.

We see a small group moving
in the channel between one building
and the next, bowing in an absent wind.

He is in a wheelchair, she is stumbling,
pushing a pram from decades ago,
coal black and wrong. There is no way
it holds a baby. Behind them,
a few more shuffling bodies in coats.

I am my own kind of damaged there,
looking out the right-hand window.
Spastic, palsied and off-balance,
I'm taking crooked notes about this place.

It is the land where he is buried, the place
she spent her whole life, the room
where they made it impossible
for her to have children.

It is the colony where he did not learn to read,
but did paint every single slat of fence
you see that shade of yellow.

The place she didn't want to leave
when she finally could,
because she'd lived there fifty years,
and couldn't drive a car, or remember
the outside, or trust anyone
to touch her gently.

And, by some accident of luck or grace,
some window less than half a century wide,
it is my backyard but not what happened
to my body—

In the Dormitory
(fall 1935)

WHERE YOU ARE (I)

Here, every season is too much of itself.
The winter comes through the break
in the windowpane and grows colder.
The snow bears on the dogwood branches
until they clatter to the ground
like felled bodies.

The summer is all sweat
and evening thunderstorms
that bring no water.
The heat warps everything wooden:
makes small mountains in the floorboards,
keeps the drawers from closing.

The doors are locked.

This is where the longest hours pass,
all these rows of narrow bunks, low lights.
One girl after another laughs,
lifts her hair from her neck,
moans in her sleep,
reaches out and brushes
someone else's shoulder.

GRAND MAL SEIZURE

There's however it is you call,
& there's whatever it is
you're calling to.

July, I sew
my own dress
from calico & lace.

August, they take it
off me in the Colony,
trade it in

for standard-issue
Virginia cotton.
Not much room

for my body in the
heavy slip; maybe
that's the idea.

For awhile the abandoning
was rare & then it was not
& would never be again.

Imagine you are
an animal in your
own throat.

The dormitory has a pitched
dark roof & a high porch.
We are not allowed outside.

Instead, we go to the window & make
a game of racing dogwood blossoms
knocked down by the wind.

Choose your flower as
it falls & see whose
is the first to hit the clay.

I beat the crippled girl every day
for a week. The trick is to pick
the smaller petals.

> *Most nights, they knot*
> *the bed sheet in my mouth*
> *so I will not bite my tongue.*

> *Lay out on the pine floor:*
> *rattle your own bones back*
> *to the center of the world.*

In the beds, the smell
of kerosene & lye.
The girls wake themselves

one after another:
spasm, whimper, whine.
Outside: cicadas.

In the distance: the bighouse lights.
Another truck comes loud up the road
bearing another girl.

There is whatever it is
you're calling to. There is
however it is you call.

LABOR

If you have the body for it, you're bound for the fields
to pick strawberries and coax the milk from cows,
or hired out to make baking powder biscuits and gravy,
to sweep floors and wash and fold a stranger's clothes.
You come back on a truck after sunset, raw and ragged, covered
in flour, tobacco, or clay. You come back bone-tired and bruised,
burned dead out and ready to be shut away. You sleep.

I know all this from stories; I do not have the body for it.
I do not go to the fields, or the barns, or the parlors of other folks' houses.
I wake at sunrise when they wake the rest, lie in bed
til somebody hauls me out and puts me by the window. Lord, I know
to want to work's a foolish thing to those who've got a body built for working.

I was as close to born here as you can get, brought twisted and mewling
to the gates and left. Since then, I am one long echo of somebody else's life.
Every understanding that I have is scrap, is shard, is secondhand.

    Distance: the space between the porch railing
        and the rise of the blue ridge.

    Water: what comes from a bucket to my body on Sundays;
        what I open my mouth for, morning and night.

    Sex: The days the girls come back smelling of whiskey,
        snuff, and sweat, and something sharp.

EVERY OTHER THING I SEE IS A GHOST

Whatever it is you were born to do   sweetheart   there's no doing it here
make peace with small labors   your own hand drawing   a needle
through a torn sheet   your elbow bending
as you soak clothes in the washroom downstairs

the storm that tears the azaleas apart along the road outside
that's it for beauty   or   also   there's the way   at night
the girls in nearby beds teach one another to cuss   whisper
goddamn it you bastard   sigh   *goddamn it all to hell*

you know   before they brought me here   I'd never seen a ghost
or anything   that wasn't really there   I'd never heard a voice
half asleep in the blackness
and had to wonder whether or not   it belonged to a body

but   after the swearing   someone has been singing me hymns from home
canan's land   *the spirit shall return   traveling on*
in the daylight   no one ever sings

sometimes   in the doorway   I think I see a hem
trailing away outside   but there's nowhere to leave to
and nobody   sweetheart   nobody has a dress that long

or lace

WITHOUT A MIND

This child is without a mind.
That one has a cave for a face
blank, unlit, and fallen in.
Back wherever she began
somebody clapped his hands
and the fire went out.
But, somehow, she continued to burn,
curling like paper tossed into the flame:
fingers, toes, and tongue drawn in
limbs pulled toward the trunk as if
wrapped tight in kitchen twine.
Some summers the cicadas shed
their brittle skin. It's just like that:
useless approximations of live things
littered on the beds as I make my rounds.
What accident of nature?
What error in material?
What sin warrants a blown brain,
a lame body? Where does it wait
to be born?

In the Blind Room
(Winter 1935)

WHERE YOU ARE (II)

There is a single chair, but often one leg is broken.
There is a single window, but often it is covered in boards.
There is no power. It is a place to forget what power is:
that a light turns on and off with the flick of a switch,
that your hand can travel that far from your body.

Sometimes, you are in the blindroom alone.
Sometimes, someone follows you in,
puts his hands around your throat.

You can feel the swollen places
in your neck, between the valleys:
forefinger and thumb,

but the thing about the darkness is
it makes things disappear.

WHAT THERE IS TO GIVE

Outside of here, my brother lost work
in the Chesapeake, and now
there is no money coming home.
Haven't you heard the news?
There is no longer enough in the world.
Not enough oil or milk, money or bread
or labor for those of us with good bodies
and sound minds. Given that,
would you load what little you have
on a boat: stack it with carrots
and sardines and silver,
then push it, unmanned,
onto the river at night?
I didn't think so.
Sometimes, when we're bringing
in a girl, I catch her face before we shut
the door and she looks almost lovely:
a useless barge lit up,
bearing away on the water.

NEW KNOWLEDGE FOR THE DARK

It's where they put you when
you run, or if they even sense
the want for fleeing in you.

In there, wherever
you came from is better.
Anywhere is better.

Hiding, freezing in your slip,
crouched in a dry creek bed,
before that, the back of a feed truck,

before that, your father's small house
& swept floors & sometimes
butter & a drawn bath.

It's important to remember that once
you had a good life. Once you did not
know how to lie in a dark room,

your cheek pressed to the floor,
peering under the doorframe,
looking for the line of light.

Once you were not waiting
to leave yourself, wanting
your skeleton shaken to pieces

so that, when it's over,
the rest of you will have nothing
at all to come back to.

In the blindroom,
there are bad days &
there are worse ones.

Once, they took me in &
there was a crack in the boards
covering the small window.

I could see the shapes of my hands
in front of me. I could put them
on the ground & think

about each finger & think
about the sky until
it happened.

Think about your body.
Think about infinity.
Think about God.

It will happen.
This is the only place
you will thank him for it.

Imagine, you have never been to the ocean
but the ocean is in you,
& sometimes, it roars.

Once, they put me in &
tied my hands behind my back
so tightly I could not feel them at all.

At first, an hour is a long time &
then an hour is not a long time at all.
It's better when they leave you there.

It's better when you can't hear
anyone's boots at the door or feel
anyone hot & oversweet above you.

Two days later, when they let me go,
my fingers were heavy stones & blue
as the bottom of the sea.

THE BLIND ROOM: AN EXECRATION

this is the beginning of the world

or   this is the world before   God made it

empty space   darkness over the deep   no sense where the edges are

I promise   it is the worst place   you've ever been

that's what I meant   the blindroom means   the world unmakes itself
in an instant   the door shuts   the sun vanishes   and with it
all the things the light makes   patterns in the dust   the dust at all
the shape of the chair   your own shadow

swallow   beetle   lightning bug   brother
all unravelled   all undone

at first   you will tell yourself stories   remember
that fall meant a bonfire   the ribcage of a buck lit up
with whatever limbs the storm brought down

old wood burns sweeter than green
the smoke stays on your skin for days   remember
your mother combing it out of your hair on the porch
your father playing banjo   then
the way the late october thunderstorm rolled in   and

drank away the stars

THE BLIND ROOM: A CONSECRATION

this is the beginning of the world

or   this is the world before   God made it

empty space   darkness over the deep   no sense where the edges are

eventually   it is the best place you've ever been

in the blindroom   the world unmakes itself
in an instant   the door shuts   the sun vanishes   and with it
all the things the light makes   fissures in the dust   the dust at all
the shape of the chair   your own shadow

sparrow   possum   sheepmoth   brother
all unraveled   all undone

at first   you will tell yourself stories   remember
you could ford a river   hold a log level
hit a long   high note   you closed your eyes to silence

after awhile   blessedly   you are the only creature
   everything is without history
there was never anyone but you in this cold   lightless place
there was never any throat but yours   never any voice
but the one you're humming with now   and that high   accompanying call
that must   thank God   be Gabriel

swallowing the final stars

AWAY

When I go, it is because they are tired of the shadow I make on the window,
the mound I make on the bed, the noise I make when they pull my dress
down over my head and it catches in my mouth and makes a gag.
It's because I drooled when they dressed my sores this week,
or I shit myself sleeping. They don't have enough bodies in the dormitory
to move me to the chair and back. Or they have too many and I'm in the way.

It will shock you, I'm sure, to know it's never because I have tried
to run anywhere. Sometimes, I do raise my good arm above my head,
and leave it there, and see if they notice.

> *Running:* I am lying in the blindness and I cannot see my body
> or the walls; maybe I am tumbling forward
> like the doctor says the planet is tumbling forward.

> *Flying:* maybe I am tumbling forward like the doctor says
> the planet is tumbling forward;
> maybe the dead weight of my left arm is a wing.

> *Faith:* maybe the dead weight of my left arm is a wing.

WHAT YOU'RE AFTER

Some of them are only imbeciles
invisibly—witless and mute—
or only partly, the drooling and shuddering
they do some hours doesn't leave a mark.
The hopelessly crippled are only good
for the clap of the belt.
But with the best ones,
it's easy to forget their lack.
They have a fine face,
long legs, a scarless stomach,
and a mouth that will open to yours
without much protest
and move like an animal.
Down there in the blackness,
held against the floor,
they are the safest thing.
They do not call you darling,
or follow you up into the light.

In the Field
(Winter 1935–1936)

WHERE YOU ARE (III)

The thing about the Shenandoah
is everything is always bending
its knees toward ruin or preparing
to rise from the ash.

Every day a whole lifetime:
in the morning the rust
of the ground is soft
and curtained in dew.

Pacing the close buildings
of the Colony, it's easy to forget
there are miles and miles
of planet outside the walls.

Whenever you can,
make yourself small
in your minor orbit,
ringed in maples

and strawberry fields,
made greater by
the mountains yawning
in and out of fog.

FAR FIELD

This month   our electricity is rationed
I am installed   hanging clothing in the first field

walking one worn gully   from the screen door to the line
            and back again
watching my shadow   scramble farther out   toward the distance
following the sun

outside   I can almost ignore the voices   they forget their language
begin   to sound the same as crows   circling a carcass
or wind whipping the gate   against the margin of my world

they've grown newly dangerous   raging and rattling the bars
as often as they sing the hymns they knew when they arrived

but they seem to depend on smallness   some close limit   for survival

when no one is looking   I pause in the gully   train my eyes
for minutes on the farthest field   there is no edge to anything
I could start running toward the distance   right now   and outpace them

in the quiet

BIRD'S-EYE

I am above, the field is below. This is one certainty of the world.
I invent every detail beyond the way it shifts in color:
    green, to bronze, to brown.

For instance, the foxes other girls report sometimes are wildly in love
and always hunting for a river. Even at night. For instance, outside,
your sweat collects the scent around it: honeysuckle, horse manure.

    Flock: the girls returning in slow shifts from the farm;
        their arms flung across each other's shoulders.

    Flinging: the loudest I can ache from the window;
        the rare moment someone tilts her face up toward me,
        hand over her eyes.

    Frost: the rare moment I don't know exactly what is coming;
        everything washed suddenly white.

WHERE YOU ARE (IV)

The thing about the Shenandoah
is everything is always
bending its knees toward ruin
or preparing to rise from the ash.

Every day a whole lifetime:
everything is loudest dying.
Evening, there is noise enough
here for a whole world.

Bats and owls and late swallows
wake up in the wind and get ready
to usher it all to its ending.
Whenever you can,

make yourself small
in your minor orbit.
Dust comes in and out
of being with the light.

In the Chapel
(Spring 1936)

WHERE YOU ARE (V)

They say every place starts to look
just like the people who move in it.

Three rows of wood pews scavenged
from bankrupt churches,
a birchbark cross leaning to the left.

The stucco on the ceiling begins to
drip a little in the heat,
and, on the table, dust
compels more dust onto the handful
of done votives and the Bible
they will not teach you to read.

PSALM

Once it was clear I would not die in early childhood,
you wheeled me out along the coach road, to the chapel, to be baptized.
Even half-wits might well have a soul to save: the concession
science makes to faith.

Whatever sins are visited upon my body,
best to do all you can to cleanse them before they ease into the air
like plague. After all, you would not want my life. Your children's children
would not want my life: stale sickness, some stranger steeling herself
to touch you if she must, and then recoiling.

The meek will inherit the earth, but you worry the mute and monstrous
will pollute it long before that happens. So you strip me down,
hold my head under the water in the basin,
count to three, and pray in every language that you know

"Dear God, bless this girl. Take her up and let her be the end of it.
Put some distance between our bodies and hers. Take her out of our hands."

     Father: Whatever force or fate has made me like this.

     Son: What will protect your daughters from a future like mine.

     Holy Ghost: You cannot hear what I am saying
               in the cathedral of my own head.

PRAYER FOR THE WRETCHED AMONG US

I.

Always, they tell you to go
where God calls you.

What they don't say is that, sometimes,
God will call you to the wilderness,

gesture toward the trees, and then
hang back and wave you on alone.

This is how I wound up granting absolution
to low-grade idiots and the worn-out women

who turn them over in bed at night and,
at dawn, go home to their own families,

try not to think of ghosts
wasting away in this world.

II.

You are not supposed to be afraid of sinners.
You should take off your shoes and give them

to the wretched and the damned.
Hold out your hand to every girl

even if she seems more animal,
statue, or remnant of plague

than lost disciple. But,
do the children of God really lose

their eyes in the backs of their heads,
and swallow their own tongues in church?

III.

I should think of her as an infant,
a baby who is saved, although

she cannot say God's name
or even understand it.

But her knees, drawn up in the washtub,
tower past her chin. I pour

Holy Water from a chipped blue pitcher,
cannot call up a prayer.

IV.

I'm glad for the twenty miles I drive
over the mountains each week,

for the latched red gate
at the mouth of Colony Road,

for the gloves I wear on days
I have to give last rites in the infirmary.

My wife is pregnant.
I am looking into the mouth of a nightmare.

Driving home in the dark,
I beg forgiveness

and louder, for protection
and the distance to forget.

THE CONVULSIONS CHOIR

They did not build
the church
for us.

I overheard one night nurse
talking to another.
They meant it for the staff

as a refuge
from the stench,
the idiot, & the insane.

They meant: you will need God
more than ever
in this place.

After all,
we are a whole host of reasons
to stop believing in anything.

I am the worst thing
the reasoned world
has wrought,

an otherwise lovely girl
daily visited by radical disorder
they say spawns somewhere

quiet & foaming
in the wounded matter
of my body & my brain.

Sundays, we are allowed in the chapel
for an hour in the morning
after the men have prayed & gone.

There are too many bodies for the pews,
so those who can all gather in the back
like starlings stunned after a storm.

I'd like to take the hands of the other
epileptic girls & lead them
up toward the altar,

humming & weaving
our arms together
like chains.

I wonder if, in concert,
we could call it up like hymns,
like speaking in tongues.

We could lie down & demand
to be raptured, or healed, to return
to safer bodies, or to dust.

As the weeks I'm here
grow achingly
to months & years

I make an outside world
of the space between
my bones.

They did not build
the church
for us.

But they leave us
alone inside it,
bar the door.

WHAT EXACTLY IS OVERHEARD

by now   there are figments   talking to me all the time
although   they still only prowl along the edges of my sight-line
pale dress   tanned hand   bell of a lip
drawn close   and then   receding like a lantern

sometimes   they remind me of peaches in summer
or a kiss   sometimes   they promise me
clean air and ease   often   they brandish a needle at my eye
and sing about the way it shines

in church   I used to laugh at folks who waltzed up the aisle
to the preacher's hand   to have a demon cast out   or swallow the Lord

now   I wonder whether the figments are living   inside my body
or beating on my chest   in search of a door

I wonder   which sounds are the real girls saying a prayer
and which   are coming from under the water in the vanishing well

Interlude

TRANSUBSTANTIATION

It's the middle of the night. I'm just a little loose on beer, and blues,
and battered air, and all the ways this nowhere looks like home:
the fields and boarded houses dead with summer, the filling station rowdy
with the rumor of another place. Cattle pace the distance between road
and gloaming, inexplicably awake. And then, the bathtubs littered in the pasture,
for sale or salvage, or some secret labor stranger than I know. How does it work,
again, the alchemy that shapes them briefly into boats, and then the bones
of great felled beasts, and once more into keening copper bells, before
I even blink? Half a mile out, the city builds back up along the margin.
Country songs cut in and out of static on the radio. Lord, most of what I love
mistakes itself for nothing.

GOING TO WATER

Now, I spend more time
in the ocean
than on land.

Often, I come back
to realize that the sun
has done a whole rotation

while I drowned.
I choke in the light &
return to the water.

> *Love, is that you there?*
> *are you waiting in the trees*
> *outside my father's house?*
>
> *Are you mimicking the voice*
> *of the mountain bluebird?*
> *Are you telling me a story?*

In my other life,
or a dream I had once
I put on a yellow dress,

left my boots in a corner,
slipped out & went
to meet you in the highest field.

I had not yet come to fear
my body, or the way it might collide
with another.

Love, is that you there?
Are you opening the doors
to stir the owls?

Are you holding a lantern?
Are you pitching the moon around
behind my eyes?

In my other life,
or a dream I had once,
I breathed air & not water,

you put your palm on the small
of my back and called it up
out of my lungs.

Now, I am the wrong
kind of creature
for this world.

Love, is that you there?

TO THAT GIRL, AS AN INFANT

I.

We were cocooned in wires
and wax paper skin,
in the same suspended half-light
of barely-alive-behind-glass.
Equal, almost girls.
I grew, but you,

you are the figure in the field
picked clean by crows
then reassembled, miniature:
fingertips for shinbones, teeth for hands
and feet, hair from the back of a neck
the fine new fuzz on your tiny little elbow head.
Baby, what becomes a body is strange.

What becomes beautiful is the wildest thing.
You are made from all that and a thicket
of thistle, a boat full of cardamom pods,
a room in a house in Virginia.
Beloved, you are held in every
improbable thing I've ever done.

II.

I hear you howl, waking
from a nightmare,
dear, disturbed little creature—
and in the light left behind
in this corner room, want you

like the breastbone excavated
from my chest.

III.

Whatever I believe about how we go on—
sometimes, watching the small, vigilant
chests of the crows in the fields,
there is only your body instead of the wound.
Love, look at the milkweed, the mountains, the dust.

In the Infirmary
(Summer 1936)

WHERE YOU ARE (VI)

There are fine metal bars on the windows, fifty metal beds.

The floor is white linoleum. The admissions rate
has been cut back to five a week to combat overcrowding.
It smells of chemicals and sweat. Every other moment
someone else begins to yell. None of this
should be at all surprising.

But this looks like
the loveliest building in the colony:
deep blue door, tall white columns,
brick trimmed in wrought-iron and kudzu.

Elsewhere, this is the year Scarlet O'Hara
falls in love with Tara. Here, the year
some fifteen hundred people
are cut open and wrecked. Mostly,
they do not know that it is happening,
that the lights going suddenly out in their windows
will never come back on.

A DICTIONARY OF HEREDITARY DEFECTS

*the comparison of idiots and normal children must almost be
a comparison between two separate species.*

It's shocking, really, how many ways
a being can go wrong before they're even born
into the world.

Cretinism: you are caught between human and animal.
Heavy and flat-faced. You have hoofs for hands,
a cow's wide tongue.

Epilepsy: you are destroying yourself from the inside out.

Feeblemindedness: I could shout into the cavern of your mouth
and hear my own words echo back off the high walls of your head,
over all the blank space of your brain. This is the most useful
noise that you will ever make.

Idiocy: you cannot even reproduce my echo.
You are living, yet already your body
has started to decay. It knows
you are not for this world.
You go limp or spastic,
turn to stone or slime.

At home, I drown the smallest kitten in
the litter. I hold its head under water
for a minute, feel its heart stop
with my thumb. It's done.

You are not for this world.
It would be cruel to let you
replicate yourself and make another

creature fated to crawl around,
feeble and stunted, yowling
for absent milk.

VIRGINIA:

BEFORE THE STATE HOSPITAL BOARD
AT

THE VIRGINIA STATE COLONY FOR EPILEPTICS AND FEEBLEMINDED

Register No.   00741   }   Order for
Inmate: Miller, Edith   }   Sexual Sterilization

Upon the petition of the State and upon consideration of the evidence introduced at the hearing of this matter, the Board finds that said inmate is

⎧ insane
⎪ idiotic
⎨ imbecile   }   and by the laws of heredity is the probable parent of
⎪ feebleminded
⎩ epileptic   X

socially inadequate offspring likewise afflicted; that the said inmate may be sexually sterilized without detriment to his / her general health, and that the welfare of the inmate and of society will be promoted by such sterilization.

Therefore, it appearing that all parties have been duly served with proper notice of these proceedings it is ordered that the operation of ⎧ vasectomy
⎨ salpingectomy   X ⎫

be performed on said inmate after not less than thirty (30) days from the date hereof

Dated: May 9th 1936

Note: Make two copies; one for guardian or committee and one for Record.

THE CLEAVING

At first,
all hands become
suddenly gentle.

More people touch you
in a single day than have touched you
in all the hours of the last, dry year.

The doctors tell you all the things
you know about yourself
as if it's news.

"You are unwell.
You are in pain.
Something is wrong."

You think that whatever is happening
after all this time is a solution
being born.

> *I will remember this day as the day*
> *I came back to my body.*
> *This time, I will anchor myself*
>
> *to my bones more firmly.*
> *You pull a boat far off the water*
> *when you know it will storm.*

They will keep you one night,
in the white of the infirmary,
patrolling your bedside,

ticking off notes on a chart,
feeling your heartbeat,
urging you to sleep

then waking you
at every hour.
In the morning,

they will say you need an appendectomy.
Only after will you have a sense that this is not
what happened, that what happened

had nothing to do with your brain,
or the water, or the rattling,
or your pain.

> *I will remember this day as the day*
> *I was cleaved from my body.*
> *Whatever they did, I am*
>
> *the silt that slips between your fingers*
> *when you dredge for the bright things*
> *at the bottom of a pond.*

VIRGINIA:

BEFORE THE STATE HOSPITAL BOARD
AT

THE VIRGINIA STATE COLONY FOR EPILEPTICS AND FEEBLEMINDED

Register No.   00816   }   Order for
Inmate: Campbell, Dorothy   Sexual Sterilization

Upon the petition of the State and upon consideration of the evidence introduced
at the hearing of this matter, the Board finds that said inmate is

insane	X
idiotic	
imbecile	
feebleminded	X
epileptic	

and by the laws of heredity is the probable parent of
socially inadequate offspring likewise afflicted; that the said inmate may be
sexually sterilized without detriment to his / her general health, and that the
welfare of the inmate and of society will be promoted by such sterilization.

Therefore, it appearing that all parties have been duly served with proper notice
of these proceedings it is ordered that the operation of { vasectomy

salpingectomy   X }

be performed on said inmate after not less than thirty (30) days from the date
hereof

Dated: July 24th 1936

Note: Make two copies; one for guardian or committee and one for Record.

WHILE UNDER

in the infirmary   the visions   grow in number
every time they take my pulse   another one

I imagine they are born in my blood   I imagine they are borne into the world

every time I take   a breath

the doctors do not tell me anything   people stopped
telling me anything   months ago

mostly I am afraid of the visions   but in the operating room
they multiply   grow gentle   sweetly   they tell me the story   of my life

once your father held you on his shoulders   so you could put your fingers
high   in the church rafters   and look for God

once you knew the name for every butterfly that flocked into the valley

I'm young   when they have told the whole story   they go back to singing

one bright morning   I'll fly away

as I wake   they tell me not to worry   with the soreness or the burning

we are everything that you will ever need to make

VIRGINIA:

BEFORE THE STATE HOSPITAL BOARD
AT

THE VIRGINIA STATE COLONY FOR EPILEPTICS AND FEEBLEMINDED

Register No. _____00895_____ } Order for

Inmate: __Carr, Frances__ } Sexual Sterilization

Upon the petition of the State and upon consideration of the evidence introduced at the hearing of this matter, the Board finds that said inmate is

insane
idiotic   X
imbecile   and by the laws of heredity is the probable parent of
feebleminded
epileptic

socially inadequate offspring likewise afflicted; that the said inmate may be sexually sterilized without detriment to his / her general health, and that the welfare of the inmate and of society will be promoted by such sterilization.

Therefore, it appearing that all parties have been duly served with proper notice of these proceedings it is ordered that the operation of { vasectomy

salpingectomy   X }

be performed on said inmate after not less than thirty (30) days from the date hereof

Dated: August 24th 1936

Note: Make two copies; one for guardian or committee and one for Record.

NUMB

Afterward, the girls to whom it's happened rehash the worst of it.
When you come back from the infirmary, for a few days
other girls will do your chores. Even the harshest few grow briefly gentle.
No one knows what happens.

It is not an appendectomy. It does not cure the pain or shaking.
Others say there is some soreness between the legs,
and then a sense, which will not leave you, that something's been undone.

I wish I could feel it in my body. Even that small burning after whatever it is
they broke would be a comfort. They do not know that I can understand
and so, nobody says a word. The only way that I can chart some change
is in the way the doctors look at me after it's happened.
Less fearful. Less appalled.

    Relief: I wake.

    Relief: upon waking, I can still lift my right arm from the bed.

    Relief: what it would mean to feel a sharpness;
        Yes, I know it happened.
        Yes, I understand that I am changed.
        Yes, I am still alive. I am still a body in the world.

In the Dormitory
(Fall 1936)

WHERE YOU ARE (VII)

Everything begins and ends here.
Still, the girls are sleeping in the narrow bunks.
Still, in their sleep, they call out.

Hey, Beloved...

Hey, Brother...

Hey, Back of Beyond...

Hey, Girl I once was long ago...

They tell you that it takes ten years of being blind
before your body gives up dreaming about sight.

Outside, the summer starts to cool.
When the trees flame into matches
the girls put their hands out
of the windows, litter the floor with leaves,
call it a map.

The birch tree's sharp leaves make one continent.
The dogwood's make another.

At night, before inspection,
they gather them up in armfuls,
and throw the whole world out the window.

OXYGEN

One woman brings her baby to work, walks with him between the aisles
of beds to be sure we are sleeping. She holds him close to her chest.
Sometimes, if the night is calm, she will reach down, touch my hand
as she passes, as if she has forgotten she does not believe I can sense it,
forgotten I was never anyone's child.

>   *Wrist:* small flawless place on my body;
>   second home of my heartbeat.

>   *Infant:* planet of heat; flawless animal;
>   what I was meant to become.

>   *Air:* thing that changes temperature,
>   tells you when another body is near.

AFTER ALL *(NOTHING)*

one morning I wake up   and the visions are bees pouring from my belly

into the globes of my eyes   someone hurls a shoe at me to stop my screaming

otherwise no one comes   I pass an hour like this

this is what no one tells you about suffering   other people visit it upon you

and then   you visit it upon yourself

AFTER ALL *(EVERYTHING)*

this morning I wake up   and for a moment   I think
    the visions have vanished

then I realize everything is shaded green   the visions have alit
    like luna moths

around the dormitory   on the doorframe   and the table   and the face

of every sleeping girl   when I blow out my breath they travel
    noiselessly into the air

I pass an hour like this   this is what no one tells you about suffering

sometimes   you would not give it up for all the world

NOTES ON THE POEMS

Although the events of this collection have an historical basis, all the figures represented here are fictional. Any resemblance to actual persons, living or dead, is purely coincidental.

Some records from The Virginia State Colony For Epileptics and Feebleminded can be found at the Library of Virginia.

Blind Room was the Colony's term for solitary confinement. Mary Bishop's article "An Elite Said Their Kind Wasn't Wanted: How Social Judgments of the Day Forced Sterilizations" in the June 26, 1994 edition of the *Roanoke Times* was especially helpful in writing the "Blind Room" section of this book.

The epigraph to "A Dictionary of Hereditary Defects" is taken from an article by Dr. Leonard Jan Le Vann in *The American Journal of Mental Deficiency*.

The Image Archive on the American Eugenics Movement through the Dolan DNA learning Center and Cold Spring Harbor Laboratory provided helpful models for the invented sterilization forms that appear in the "Infirmary" section.

ACKNOWLEDGMENTS

Thank you to the editors of the following journals, in which many of these poems first appeared, sometimes in slightly altered form:

The Adroit Journal: "Where You Are (vii)"; "Oxygen"
Colorado Review: "The Cleaving", "While Under"; "Numb"; "A Dictionary of Hereditary Defects"
Connotation Press: An Online Artifact: "Where You Are (ii)"; "What There Is To Give"; "New Knowledge For The Dark"; "The Blind Room: An Execration"; "The Blind Room: A Consecration"; "Away"
Gulf Coast: "Grand Mal Seizure"; "Labor"; "Every Other Thing I See Is A Ghost"; "Without a Mind"
Meridian: "Transubstantiation"

*

I'm indebted to an extraordinary collection of teachers and mentors who helped shepherd me as a young writer: Taije Silverman, Margo Figgins, Brendan Matthews, Peter Filkins, Ian Bickford, Asma Abbas, Brittany Perham, Molly Antopol, Eavan Boland, Louise Glück. None of these poems would be possible without them.

I'm particularly grateful to my teachers at the University of Mississippi, Derrick Harriell, Dave Smith, and Ann Fisher Wirth, whose wise and careful counsel was indispensable in shaping and revising this manuscript. Inexpressible gratitude, especially, to Beth Ann Fennelly, whose guidance, faith, and friendship have made all the difference. Thank you for knowing where I belonged long before I did.

Jim Magnuson believed in this manuscript when it—and I—were still an awful mess. Kate Daniels and Mark Wagenaar gave me generous and essential feedback on these poems.

So many dear friends were devoted and brilliant readers for this manuscript as it developed. Thanks to Laura Eve Engel, Taya Kitaysky, Heather McLeod, Emily Rials, and Virginia Henry. Thanks, too, to my colleagues at

75

the University of Mississippi, who patiently and insightfully responded to many of these poems.

For the kind of friendship that keeps you alive, I am so, so lucky to have Molly Gail Shannon, Torry Castellano, Josh Francis, Aaron Thayer, and Kate Sparks. I love you all.

To Alana Levinson-LaBrosse: Thank you for the trip that gave rise to this project.

Susannah Nevison's and Allison Seay's poems have been keeping me company since long before I was lucky enough to know the poets who wrote them, and they gave me hope there might be a home for this book in the world.

Many thanks to John and Renée Grisham, whose generous fellowship provided me the time and space to complete these poems, and to the Lexi Rudnitsky Poetry Project and Persea Books for believing in this collection and bringing it to life. Special thanks to my editor, Gabriel Fried, for his wisdom, humor, and keen eye.

Thank you, above all, to my family, in all its iterations:

to Helen and Bruce Dixon, for their unwavering and unquestioning support, and to Tim, Joanna, Kate, and Sarah McCully for their love.

Craig, Sheila, Julia, Eleanor, and Margot: thank you for loving me through every stage of my life and for holding me steady whether I was laughing or crying.

Olivia and Walker, I couldn't have asked for better siblings, teammates, or partners in crime.

To my parents, Carrie and John Gregory Brown: first teachers, readers, editors, fiercest advocates, beloved friends. Without you, none of this.

THE LEXI RUDNITSKY FIRST BOOK PRIZE IN POETRY

The Lexi Rudnitsky First Book Prize in Poetry is a collaboration between Persea Books and The Lexi Rudnitsky Poetry Project. It sponsors the annual publication of a collection by an American woman who has yet to publish a full-length poetry book.

Lexi Rudnitsky (1972–2005) grew up outside of Boston. She studied at Brown University and Columbia University, where she wrote poetry and cultivated a profound relationship with a lineage of women poets that extends from Muriel Rukeyser to Heather McHugh. Her own poems exhibit both a playful love of language and a fierce conscience. Her writing appeared in *The Antioch Review, Columbia: A Journal of Literature and Art, The Nation, The New Yorker, The Paris Review, Pequod*, and *The Western Humanities Review*. In 2004, she won the Milton Kessler Memorial Prize for Poetry from Harpur Palate. Lexi died suddenly in 2005, just months after the birth of her first child and the acceptance for publication of her first book of poems, *A Doorless Knocking into Night* (Mid-List Press, 2006). The Lexi Rudnitsky First Book Prize in Poetry was founded to memorialize her and to promote the type of poet and poetry in which she so spiritedly believed.

Previous winners of the Lexi Rudnitsky First Book Prize in Poetry:

2015	Kimberly Grey	*The Opposite of Light*
2014	Susannah Nevison	*Teratology*
2013	Leslie Shinn	*Inside Spiders*
2012	Allison Seay	*To See the Queen*
2011	Laura Cronk	*Having Been an Accomplice*
2010	Cynthia Marie Hoffman	*Sightseer*
2009	Alexandra Teague	*Mortal Geography*
2008	Tara Bray	*Mistaken for Song*
2007	Anne Shaw	*Undertow*
2006	Alena Hairston	*The Logan Topographies*